The Book:

About This Book

This is not your average read. This is a book of self expression. It is a visual representation of how I have seen myself and how I let my feelings take over. The pages became my safe space where I could be open and vulnerable. This book expresses personal details though the form of poems, monologues and free speech. Growing up, I was very shy and reserved. I kept everything bottled up. But I realized that I can't keep hiding how I feel. So I started writing it out. Writing became my therapy. I pray that upon reading this book, that you not look at it as a cry for help, but a cry for understanding. I see things in different perspectives. No hate. Only love. To the readers of this book, this is a judgment free zone. When you open this book, you open my heart. My soul flows through the pages. My heart is in every line. I have become vulnerable. I have become an open book. I have made the decision to share a little of myself with you. The highs and lows. My thought process. How I see the world. This is it. Now you see me.

The Author:

I'm just an average quiet black girl who decided to speak up. I realized that I am not the only one trying to get through life with mental set backs. I want to reach out to the ones who feel misunderstood and alone. I wanted this book to be a diary of self expression, reflection, and love. I hope it helps to know that someone else understands.

Dear Lord,

    May the person reading this find a connection and find help through You. Help them be inspired to write out their feelings as well. Use me as a tool for the one who is struggling with how they feel. Let the release happen for them as it did for me. I thank You for the motivation to be brave enough to put myself out for there world to see. I thank You Lord because there is healing through the pain. Let the people find their healing as well.

In Jesus Name Amen

Unbottled

Short Stories, Poems, and Monoluges

By

Danae Henry
Cover art by Nicholas Lievers

Papyrus Author, Inc. - Virginia Beach

Table of Contents

Chapter One : Now You See Me pg. 5
Visual
The Inner Monologue
Bloom
Shame
Heartbreak
Breathe
Sad Black Girl
Cope
Ephesians 6:10-18
Finding Stability
My Turn
Wanted
Behind The Scenes
I Stay Still
Message In a Bottle
They Can't Hear Me
T.B.H.
Emotional
Blind
Black Lives Matter

Chapter Two : Down The Rabbit Hole pg.42
Imagination vs. Reality
Depression
Trapped

Guilt
Alone
Imaginary Me
Optimistic
Judgment
Alone Again
Battle of Me
The Afterthought
Rage
Perfection
Cracked
Fear
Consumed
The Change
Triggered

Chapter Three : Life pg. 78
Out Of Hiding
Little Girl
Awkward
Introvert
My Skin
New School
Young "Love"
Loss
Duffy
College
Fibroids
In That Moment
Thoughts of Suicide
The Man After Gods Own Heart

P.U.S.H
The Virus that Shook the World
2020
Emotional

Chapter Four: Love Letters pg. 119
I John 4:16,21
Dear Younger Me
Thankful
Way Maker
Psalm 8:3-5
Self Love
II Corinthians 1:3,4
Mother
The Open Door
A Vow
Blessed
Let Go
I Love Me
Affirmations
Now It's Your Turn

For You:

If you have not been through mental set-
backs,
This is not for you.
If you don't agree with therapy,
This is not for you.
If you have never felt judged,
This is not for you.
If you've never felt alone,
This is not for you.
This book is for the outcast.
This book is for the loners.
This book is for the broken.
This book is for the ones looking for some-
one who will listen.
This book is for the lost.
This book is for the ones who felt like giv-
ing up.
You are not alone. This book is for you.

Chapter One : Now You See Me

Visual

I have always had a hard time with

public speaking. But I yearned to have my

voice heard. I find it easier to express

myself through writing. I want to reach

out and connect through words. I want to

tell stories that trigger the imagination. I

want to paint the picture with language.

Make the words visual, set the stage and

draw the story with letters. The words are

illustrations. As I write it, I envision it. I

see the paint strokes through my key pad.

This is my therapy. All the words I'm too

shy to speak are here, on this paper. My

pages speak for me. I am now an open

book. The introvert speaks.

The Inner Monologue

I'm fine.

I'm just fine.

Don't worry about me,

I'll be okay. See.

Oh, these tears,

I'm just a little tired,

I just yawned that's all.

Yes I'm sure.

I don't need your help...wait.

No, never mind.

No it's nothing. I don't want to bother you with it.

It's stupid.

It's not important.

No really, I'm just over emotional, that's it.

I'm overreacting again.

It's not as serious as it seems.

It's all in my head.

I'm okay. Honest.

I'm alright I'll be fine, like always.

I'll feel better tomorrow.

I promise. I just need to be alone.

I just need some time.

But,

Could you just, stay here for a minute?

Can I just cry for a second?

Then I'll be okay.

No questions,

no judgment,

no words.

Just let me express this.

I'll let you in.

I'll let you take a peek.

I'll tell you the things that make me tick.

No questions,

No judgment.

Just me and my thoughts. Ready?

Here we go.

My hearts beating fast,

or is it slow, I don't know.

I want to scream.

No, don't scream, keep it in, I'm alright.

I'm fine,

I'm okay,

I'll get over it, I'll feel better tomorrow.

I will be alright.

I'll just wait for tomorrow.

Waiting, waiting for it to be over.

Some nights I close my eyes and imagine

I'm someone else.

Someone powerful and confident.

I imagine the story with vivid detail.

I take flight into the fictional stories of my

childhood.

I am whoever I want to be.

Then I wake up.

I come back to my reality.

Back to life.

Simple, yet difficult.

Comfortable, yet overbearing.

At times, too much to maintain.

But I stay in control.

There are lessons to learn.

People are looking at me.

Waiting for me to make a move.

"Will she pass? Will she fail?"

Will I live, will I die?

Options.

Will I be like my mom or my dad?

Am I pretty or am I plain?

Am I enough?

Answers I wish I knew.

Thoughts run across my head daily,

Make me question who I am.

Just another quiet black girl,

wondering through life,

Making it up as she goes.

Creating a cycle.

Waiting,

Waiting for it to be over.

Bloom
Everyone is ahead of you, but it's okay.
It may take longer to get there for you.
But you will make it, do not stop.
Don't quit now you're almost there.
It may look like your in last place, but
when you bloom, they'll all be old news.
This is your show, don't let them slow you
down.
Focus.
Focus.
Focus on your dream.

Focus on your talent.
Channel your skills.
Don't look back.
Look forward, look up, it's okay.
You're gonna make it.
Slow and steady, wins the race.
Practice makes perfect.
Your hard work will prosper.
The wait will surely be worth it.
Before you know it.
You will Bloom.

Shame

Shame on me, yes, shame on me.

Shame on me, not shame on you.

Shame on me for falling for you,

For thinking you were the one.

Shame on me for believing it.

Shame on me for thinking you where

Batman when you were the Joker.

Shame on me for thinking it would work.

I was almost your Harley Quinn.

Shame on me for thinking about our future.

I was the fool, so shame on me.

I fell for your clever ways and smooth talk

like butter.

Not knowing it would turn into a knife.

I fell for it, so shame on me.

You only did what you knew.

Shame on me for trying to look pass the

fault and find a realer you.

But you were already you.

Shame on me for being open and gullible.

Shame on me for letting my guard down and taking a chance.

Shame on me, yes, shame on me.

Heartbreak

I left my heart in the wrong ally. The street name was Broken rd. When I found it, it was out of shape, bent, shattered and abused. I had to nurse it back to health. I needed to heal my own heart before I could let anyone else see it. I tried to walk it off, told myself I was over it. But I was lying to myself, lying to my heart. Letting the open wound get infected. I had to stop the cycle, go on hiatus. Spiritually find myself again. I had to visit the broken heart hospital and let a professional look after it. I received

my healing, took my time, played it safe. I

told myself I would never let my heart get

that abused ever again. I guarded it,

patrolled it and took care of every wound. I

became over protective. I became afraid. I

expected the worse. I never wanted to let

my guard down again. Years went by and I

felt my guard slip. The walls I put around

my heart started cracking. Out of fear of

losing control, I quickly retaliated. I didn't

think my heart was ready to be exposed. I

didn't want to lose it again. I protected my

self. But my heart longed to love again. So

I took a chance, let's see where it goes.

Breathe

I breathe in.

I breathe out.

I start.

I finish.

Day in, day out.

Breathe in, Breathe Out.

A life of silence.

A life of observance.

I see the world, It watches and waits.

Breathe In, Breathe Out.

Watching, waiting, listening, never

speaking.

Only breathing.

All my life.

Only breathing.

UNBOTTLED

My heart is beating, racing, yearning.

Its drowned out by the sound of breathing.

"Speak up", the mind says, "they need to

hear your voice".

I open my mouth,

nothing.

Breathe in, Breathe Out.

Maybe tomorrow.

I'll do it tomorrow,

but today,

I'll breathe in,

breathe out.

And soon.

I will speak.

Sad Black Girl

Sometimes, I feel like being sad. But if I do, people can take it the wrong way or pressure me until I tell them what's wrong. So I stay happy and cheerful to keep from showing the sadness that is slowly consuming my life. Sometimes, I want to tell everyone. I want to scream from the mountain tops all my issues and problems, but it's not that easy. I pray and pray till my tears soak the pillows. How can I know God hears me? Many times I've felt left out or rejected because I was different. I have learned from my past experiences. They have made me who I am today. Insecure, shy, afraid. It's hard to see now because I have worked hard to hide it. I am an

emotional wreck. A sad black girl, trying to

make the best of life. Waiting for her big

break. Waiting to be heard. Tired of being

misunderstood. Inwardly screaming. Crying

in the shadows.

Cope

I sit in my bed a lot,
Letting my thoughts roam free.
I'm not sure how to control them.
Sometimes I'm up, sometimes I'm down.
It's a mental roller coaster.
I'm not sure how to explain it to others.
I'm scared they'll treat me different.
They'll think I'm crying for attention.
I keep it to myself.
But when I do that it gets worse.

My thoughts turn into emotions that burst
out of me uncontrollably.
I become immersed in a false reality.
My negative mentality takes control of me.
In the form of tears it takes me.
I'm caught up in fear, guilt, and past
mistakes.
I'm overwhelmed by loneliness, paranoia,
and low self-esteem.
All of this emotion, over a mere over
reaction, to a thought.
How do I control this part of me?
How do I control my mind.
I don't want to go insane.
I want to live outside of my head.
I find ways to cope.
I look at how others cope.
I see how they handle their emotions.
Some people drink it away.
I tried to drink it away.

I wish I could drown out thought and feeling.

Lose all self-control.

But in the morning it all comes back.

Reality hits like a hangover brick.

Some people smoke it away.

They breathe in calm and breathe out the feeling.

The high takes over and settles them.

It only gives a temporary peace.

A peace I would long to have permanent.

Some people take medicinal routes.

They can be natural or over the counter.

Peace and calmness, wrapped in a bottle.

Some people spend a lot of money,

To keep that constant peace steady.

Some people don't cope at all.

They let their emotions take control.

They let their mental health become toxic.

Some seek and confide in professional help.

They help them understand who they are.
Allowing them to look inside themselves.
Seeing what's real and what's not.
Everyone finds a way to cope.
We all need a little help.
So, that little thought won't become a
mental set back.
My mental health is important to me.
I'll find help, cope, be myself and be better.
Until my little thoughts don't own me
anymore.

Ephesians 6:10-18.

"Finally, my brethren, be strong in the

Lord, and in the power of his might. Put on

the whole armor of God, that ye may be

able to stand against the wiles of the devil.

For we wrestle not against flesh and blood,

but against principalities, against powers,

against the rulers of the darkness of this
world, against spiritual wickedness in high
places. Wherefore take unto you the whole
armor of God, that ye may be able to
withstand in the evil day, and having done
all, to stand."

Finding Stability

Wake up.

Eat.

Work.

Sleep.

Repeat.

Don't forget they need you.

Push and pull.

Don't forget to smile.

Stay positive.

Don't let them see they've got to you.

No tears.

Finding stability within the chaos.

Lord, grant me peace.

When I don't feel like waking up,

When the inspiration doesn't come.

Lord, send Your Spirit.

So I may be encouraged.

I need Your stability.

My Turn

I find myself asking, "when is it my turn" a

lot. I see everyone growing around me. I

watch in awe as they shine. Then I whisper

to myself, can I be next? I am working

towards it and building myself up. Mentally

preparing for when my moment comes.

The problem is that I keep stumbling, I

scare myself into doubt. I'm trying to trust

the process, but I'm fearful of the journey.

I want what's best for me and I'm not sure

how to get to it. It's so close yet so far.

Sometimes I give up mentally. I get

depressed. I fall into a pattern. Then I find

myself having to repent and start all over

again. I'm waiting for my turn. Patiently

waiting to been heard. Patiently waiting to

be understood. Patiently waiting for the

moment. Writing, wishing, praying, waiting.

My turn is coming. I'm next.

Wanted

I can feel it.

I know the feeling. To know when you're

not wanted. To be looked down at. I've

been the one no one wants on their team.

I've been the outcast. I am a loner. I don't

ask for your company. I'll just sit by myself

if need be. Unwanted, unneeded. Disliked.

Judged. They assume my character. They

don't like me. So I don't like them. I don't

need you anyway. I'm too boring for you.

I'm not old enough. I'm not loud and

obnoxious enough. I'm not black enough

for you. I'm not like everyone else. It

offends you that I don't want to be. I'm

different. You don't like it. I'm too soft. Too

shy. Stuck up. I can't do anything right.

That's what you think of me. So you ignore

me. You make me feel unwanted. I go

home and wonder what's wrong with me. I

cry it out because I'm a cry baby. That

offends you as well. There's just no

pleasing you. I use to wonder, if I just ran

away, what would you do. Would anyone

care? If I just died. Would you cry for me?

Would you miss me? Would you want me

then? I begged for your attention. But I

was shunned and ignored. So I locked

myself away. Locked up my emotions. I

closed myself off from the world. I went

rouge. Since no one cared, I didn't care

either. Unwanted, unloved, ignored,

judged. This was the lie I believed. My

mind blocked out my worth. The past is a

dark place that haunts me. These

memories haunted me. I will not let them

haunt me anymore. I am loved. I have

found people that care about me. I am

wanted.

Behind the Scenes

I do my best work behind the scenes.

 You never realized it was me.

Silently help,

I don't make it known.

I want my actions to be louder.

I don't want to tell you what I can do.

I want to show you.

Your unaware of my small gestures,

my little random acts of kindness.

But as soon as I rest,

you see me as unproductive.

I work behind the scenes.

I go unnoticed.

Easily forgotten.

I do my best work alone.

I Stay Still

Pressure. Crushed with pressure.

Expectations. So much expectation. I don't

know what to do. Feeling overwhelmed

with pressure. Pressure for kids, marriage,

a career...I want to escape the pressure. I

want to tell you so badly that yes

everything is gonna happen but I don't know when. Waiting. Everyone around me is flourishing. I stay still. Their lives grow. I stay still. They move forward. I stay still. I want to move. But I stay still. Is there something wrong with me??? Why can't I move with them. Why am I always left behind. I want to move too. But, I stay still. I want so many things. My dreams seem so hard to reach. I think I'm close, but then I'm not. I get set back. I get depressed. Then I have to restart myself. I have to motivate myself. I need to push myself out of this stillness. I must move. I don't want to stay still. I can not stay still.

Message In a Bottle

I take it all in.

Unbothered.

I take the hits.

I feel the rejection.

I keep in my reaction.

I listen to your negativity.

But I don't let it get to me.

I bottle it up.

It stays inside.

The things I could have said.

The clap backs I should have uttered.

All of it stayed in a bottle.

I took each pain.

Every unfair thought.

All of my emotions.

I put them in a bottle.

It was safe, so I thought.

Year by year, the bottle would crack.

My ability to bottle my feelings grew weak.

I could not keep it in anymore.

Tears overflew the bottle making hard to fit

anything else in.

The bottle is full.

It is breaking.

I must find a way to maintain my sanity.

The bottle has burst.

Out comes my resented thoughts.

Out comes the emotions of the past.

Out comes the guilt.

All of my fears have become reality.

I must find a way to rebuild my sanity.

The bottle is broken.

The messages have found there way out.

Everything I bottled up has now exploded.

Now I must find a way to put myself back

together again.

They Can't Hear Me

If I screamed at the top of my lungs, would

you hear me then?

If I became so brutally honest, would it

hurt your feelings?

Would you hear me then?

But what if I became reckless and unruly,

would you hear me then?

I try to be calm, but they can't hear me.

I try to be polite, but they can't hear me.

I try to be nice, open, accommodating, but

they can't hear me.

I'm too quiet, too shy.

I go unnoticed, I stay in the background.

They can't see me, They can't hear me.

T.B.H

To be honest, I don't know my next move.

I'm not sure of my purpose,

I don't know where I'm going.

To be honest, I don't want to be a burden

to you.

I don't want to worry you.

But I don't want to be alone.

To be honest, I'm afraid.

I'm scared to let go.

And I fear that I may fail you.

Just to be honest, I'm trying.

I'm trying to make you happy.

But honestly I'm not happy.

Emotional

I cry too long. I care too hard. I over-think

the situation. My hormones take over. I

overreact. I take things way too seriously.

Why do I beat myself up like this? Why

must my first instinct be worry? What do I

fear? The consequences of failure and

defeat. Having the guilt of making the

wrong decision haunt me all of my life. My

mind automatically sets up the negative

scenario in my head that makes anxiety overcome me. I am paralyzed by it. It sweeps me into tears of fear. I am enthralled by my emotions so much it turns into panic. My breathing is obnoxious but I can't control it. I try to calm down but the smallest negative thought will send me right back into it. I look foolish. But it has to come out. I have to cry. I have to realize the emotion. My body is purging it out of me. I am an emotional being. When I try to hold my feelings in, they come back in full force. I've tried holding them in before. Maybe that's why my cries seem more hysterical than they should. They could be worse. My emotions could take me out if I don't take care of them properly. Please let me feel what I'm feeling. Let me go through my process. My emotions are valid. They are a part of me. You think I am weak because of it. I feel things more intensely than you do. I feel other peoples emotions as well. I have compassion for others going through. I understand the struggle of feeling hurt, alone, lost, and confused. It's okay to cry sometimes. It's okay to feel your emotions. If you try to control them now, you won't be able to control it later. Cry, breathe, then let it go.

Blind

So tell me, how long have you been blind?

I've been showing the signs since five.

Fear, anxiety, insecurity. Why can't you see

it? I didn't know then but now I understand

me. But why can't you? I just needed you

to hold my hand. I just wanted to be

comforted. Help me out, please. Tell me

I'm alright. That this will past. Just

understand me. I'm trying my best to

figure out life. I'm trying to find where I fit.

I just need that extra encouragement.

Make me laugh to keep from crying. Hold

me close so I feel comfort. Is it too much

to ask? Am I being too selfish? Am I too

needy? Or would you rather stay blind to

my silent cry. My desperate quiet call. The
signs were all there. You just couldn't see
it.

Black Lives Matter

From slavery to oppression, to civil rights,

to equal rights. From lynching, to police

brutality, to racism. We've seen poverty,

death, pain, injustice, rioting, chaos,

confusion, hate, prejudice, fear and loss.

We have witnessed how hard it is for a

young black man or women to survive

without getting caught by the crooked cop.

We have been falsely accused of being a

threat as soon as we come out the womb.

We are born with the fear of not living a full

life. Our lives are in consent danger when
we step out the house. No matter what we
say, how we say it, how compliant we are,
or how well-spoken we are. Time after time
we are knocked down. We are provoked to
anger. Our voices are drained out by
teargas. Our emotions boil over. Our
dreams are lost. We are condemned to a
nation that refuses to admit to their flaws.
The color of our skin has made us not
matter. We are cast out and put down like
the natives of whom this land was stolen
from. Our Black Lives Matter, but they can't
seem to wrap their heads around that. If
you came down from your pride, and take
the planks out of your eyes, maybe you

could see us. Maybe you could understand

why Martin marched, why Malcolm

revolted, and why Colin took a knee. We

are not some pets you control. We have

hearts, souls, and beautiful minds. We

want to be treated equally and fairly. We

don't want to die.

Chapter Two : Down The Rabbit Hole

Imagination vs. Reality

I am a magical being. I have powers beyond the imagination. One of my powers is invisibility. I have it mastered. I can be undetectable. This power helps me avoid social awkwardness. I can hide from confrontation and uncomfortable situations with ease. I've had this power for as long as I can remember. I accidentally used it when I was younger at a water park. My parents where frantic. We never stepped foot in that park again. I can disappear so easily. I have also created my own world.

It's my place of peace and magic. Anything

can happen here. There are mermaids,

fairies, and even vampires. They all live in

my world. I can be who ever I want to be

too. I am at peace here. The world makes

sense when I am here. Nothing bothers

me. I am impenetrable. As long as I stay in

my world. My imagination. I realized when

I was younger, how innocent and free I use

to be. My imagination was endless. I

wanted to do everything and be

everything. My set back was always my

shyness. In my room I was invincible,

fearless, and confident. But outside, I

withdrew from those feelings. I

daydreamed and imagined spin-offs and

sequels from my favorite shows and movies. At a young age I enjoyed creating my own stories. The problem was I always kept it to myself. I had drawings and stories and even backstories for my own characters. I loved to create new adventures. I could spend a whole day creating a story that would forever stay in my head. I was afraid that it was impossible for me to enter that world and create Disney hits or Blockbuster movies. I was afraid of being turned down or ignored. So it became a way I coped with my life. I loved watching T.V. All the different shows and peoples creations coming to life. It inspired my creative side, I just never quite

knew how to get there. I also wanted to fly.
I wished and dreamed that pixie dust was
real. I wanted Tinker Bell and Peter Pan to
come in and take me to Never land. So
many wild and bold thoughts. I wished that
Disney had found me and wanted my input
and ideas. It was and still is my dream. My
only set back was my fear of public
speaking. I will have my moment where I
can finally speak in front of people and not
feel nervous or start shaking. I always beat
myself up about why I can't just get up
there and say what I need to say but when
I get up there I choke. I have to force
myself to be bold. It's a mental battle when

I go upfront and no one even realizes how much of an emotional strain it is.

Depression

So, I have felt depressed for a long time. I have spent my time looking for approval or acknowledgment in other people. I have struggled with loving myself. I've always felt like I haven't accomplished much. I've always been sensitive and a push over as well. I have been bottling up emotions so much that I fear I might lose control of my actions. Lord, please don't let me lose control. I've been pushed passed my breaking point on many different occasions to a point that I've considered running away or self harm. I'm too scared to kill myself, but I've felt like I just want to be gone. There's that feeling you get when you want to escape, but you don't know how. So you feel trapped. I keep wondering why am I'm still here. All a wanted was a "your doing a good job", or a "how are you feeling today". Just to have someone who genuinely cares about me. Not to feel like I'm a screw up. I keep thinking I'll be lost and alone forever. How come it's so easy for everyone to get over it and I just can't? I tell myself to let it go, and I do, but it just finds its way right back. Maybe I'm just tired. Maybe I'm overreacting. I get so worked up, then everyone goes about their business and I'm the one looking dumb with tears, red puffy eyes and snot coming down my face. I feel like I'm just here for other people, but when is it gonna be for me. I have dreams, goals and things and places I want to see. I long for freedom. A day where no one tells me what to do, or where to go. I pray for freedom but I still feel trapped. Locked in a cage where the bars are just wide enough for me to reach my arm through, but that's it. I wanna get out but I don't know how.

Trapped

Stuck, I fear being stuck. Not being able to get out. Having to stay in one place forever. I am afraid that I will never break out. I am vulnerable. They see me now, for the sham that I am. A useless thing. I am nothing. Stuck in a nothing. Where can I go? I run through the halls and stairways. There are doors everywhere, but I can't open them. Every last door is locked. I am frantic, yanking at the knobs. I push and kick, but they do not budge. I am desperate, running to the next door, and the next. I'm trying to escape. It seems impossible. No door will open for me. Is this my life? A world of closed doors. When will it open? Am I ever getting out of here? There is a light at the end of the hallway. A bright blue door out of nowhere. I walk down the long hallway. Nervous and anxious at what lies at the end of hall, but I continue my steady pace. I approach the blue door. It is a vibrant blue door with detailed carvings of various flowers. The door knob is golden. I reach for it. I wake up.

Guilt

I pray for guidance to get me out. I pray for peace in the midst of my storm. And I pray for my life, that I will keep fighting for it. Some days I don't want to. I

want to run away but I have nowhere to
go, so I'm just stuck here. Feeling alone
and mentally abused. Feeling like my only
usefulness is giving and not getting. I'm
praying away the guilt of my life and the
shamefulness of my past. Years ago I was
naive and stupid, and the fear of that
coming to the light still haunts me to this
day. Don't ask me about it because I don't
like to talk about it. It's embarrassing to
admit your faults. I'm not bold enough. My
self-confidence is low and I'm just trying to
pull it back up. I try to pray the shame
away, I wish it never happened. Everyday I
wish that never happened. I've heard the
phrase all the time, everything happens for

a reason. I guess I had to learn the hard way. Or maybe I have not yet realized its meaning. Self-worth maybe. Knowing how to respect myself or knowing the difference between someone who respects you and someone who does not.

Alone

I don't want to be by myself. I don't always like the quiet. If it gets too quiet, my mind starts to lose it. I don't like being by myself for long periods of time. No one checks on me. No calls. No one asking how am I doing. I just want you to have time for me. I don't like having to sit alone, go out alone or eat alone. I don't like the extra space. I want someone to worry about me.

Everyone is too busy for me. I feel like an

afterthought. I don't want to stay here

alone. Take me with you. I don't like the

feeling. I don't want it. It's too quiet.

Please, if its only for five minutes, I just

need some type of social interaction. Being

alone isn't fun. Can I just have a few

minutes of your time. Don't leave me

alone. Please. Its aches. I feel like nothing.

I feel like a loser. Like nobody even cares.

My minds not set up for this. The quiet gets

to me. I feel like I'm losing my sanity. Then

the breakdown sets. And I cry to fill the

void. I turn on the T.V. so the noise fills the

void. Breathe. Play a game, and relax.

Ignore the fact that you're alone. They'll be here soon. Everyone's just working. Their all busy. But they will make time for you. Breathe. It won't be like this forever. Take advantage of this loneliness while you have it.

Imaginary Me

Once upon a time, I felt empty. So I created another me to make up for that emptiness. She had everything that I lacked. She was brave, confident, and beautiful. She could do anything she put her mind to. Her only weakness was being stuck in my head. Every now and then, she would find ways to get out of my head. I felt like I could be this imaginary persona.

She could start a good conversation and

keep people engaged in what she would

say. She could speak easily without

stumbling over words and forgetting the

topic. She could stand up for herself, and

what's right. She was a go-getter that

could make friends and network with ease.

She would never be afraid. She would

never feel vulnerable. She wouldn't care

how others would treat her or judge her.

Oh, how I wish I could let her out

completely. I daydream about her. I want

to be like her someday. Someday, I'll finally

let her shine.

Optimistic

I'm alone. But I have time to think. A
moment to process. The space is open, free
roam. No one to judge. No one to tell me
no. I need to use this time wisely. Write
down every idea. Focus on the goals that
need to be taken care of. Breathe and take
it easy. I am where I need to be.
Everything happens for a reason. When no
one is here, I sing. I fill the space with my
mediocre voice. It's fairly good. I can carry
a note. Hold it and shape it. Just practicing
confidence. I dance when no ones
watching. I practice what I want to teach. I
could do a little dancing If I really wanted
to. Yes I can dance but my legs can't

stretch that far. Yes I can keep up but I can't bend that way. I draw a lot. I'm pretty good. Its something I could really build on. It takes so much time and concentration. If I don't keep up with the talent, I have to re-teach myself. It isn't hard. It's just so much focus. In the time that I have, I must focus on my talents. I must concentrate. So much that needs to be done. I can do this.

Judgment

I'm black, so they assume I should act a certain way. I have curves, so they stare too long. They make me uncomfortable. They think I look "stuck up" based on simply my looks. I get mugs and mean glares from women. I get stares and cat-calls from men. I don't like the attention. I look down. I look away. Avoid the crowd. Avoid the eyes. Avoid the judgment. I don't travel alone often. It makes me feel uncomfortable. I feel their eyes. Watching me. And then they judge. Quickly trying to tell me who I am. I wasn't black enough, so they called me an "Oreo". I grew up in a good home, so they called me spoiled. I was too quiet so they called me weird. So much judgment. If you got to know me, you would understand. You didn't want to understand. So I became the weird little black girl that no one understood. You judged me before I could speak. You didn't

let me tell you my interests, hobbies, likes

and dislikes. I fell under your judgment. I

could have been the mean girl. I could

have hurt a lot of people. I could have

rolled my eyes and snapped right back. I

kept my mouth shut for a reason. If I said

what I really felt, I could have made you

cry. I could have clapped back. I could

have mean mugged you too. But I wanted

you to like me. You were so quick to point

out my flaws, but if I did the same, I'd be

the mean one. I could have fought you.

You talked too much. But I kept it to my

self. Because, I wanted you to like me. You

didn't like me ether way. I'm not dumb. I

know when I'm not wanted. That's why I
didn't talk to you. I don't want to hang out
with you, since you made me feel
unwanted. I don't care anymore. I don't
want to be where I'm not wanted. I'd
rather be left alone. Judge all you want,
but there is only one judgment that
matters to me.

Alone Again

I sit here, in this quiet space. No one is
here with me, holding me, comforting me.
My friends are gone. There is no laughter
or talking. Only silence and the sound of
my breathing. I am alone. I can turn on the
T.V., browse my phone, but then, I'm

forced to see the reality of how ignorant
this country has become. I try to keep
myself from, spiraling down into that,
place. I was once comfortable, but the
world wasn't as crazy as it was when I was
young. It seems like America has split up
into two sides. It's so much happening. I
shut myself out. And then, that's when I
start thinking. Then I realize how dark life
can be. Forced to see myself, to hear my
thoughts. I think I'm alone. But I feel like
I'm not alone. I feel like I'm alone. But I
think, I'm not alone. I wish I was alone.
Every day its something else. Pick someone
up here , take another to the store, drop
one more off here, its an endless cycle that

I just want to stop. Leave me alone! Do it yourself! I'm tired. But to them, I'm just here for their benefit. I'm such a big help. But I need help too. Don't they know? No, because the minute I lay my head down and tell them I can't, I'm lazy, ungrateful, selfish. I just want them to leave me alone. I just want to be left alone for maybe a day, or a week, or a whole month. So I can have time for my self. Is that too much to ask. Well, is it? I don't know. I keep getting asked the same questions. "What do you plan on doing with your life?" "How are you going to make any money?" "How are you gonna make it out here?" I just started responding with I don't know. They then look at me with discontent and confusion.

They act like their the ones who paid for

my tuition. I'm still learning. I'm still trying

to figure out my path.

The Battle of Me

I must get out of bed.

I must face the day.

But I'd rather not.

I want to sleep it away.

I want to disappear.

But they're relying on me.

I must persevere.

I have to get up.

I have to show them I can do this.

I must get up.

I'll put a mask over my frown.

Please don't look at me.

I will look down.

I keep feelings to myself.

Smile, be cordial.

Ignore my mental health.

Pretend to be happy.

My true self makes you uncomfortable.

Pretend to be happy.

I feel ignored.

Pretend to be happy.

Laugh to keep from crying.

Pretend to be happy.

I feel so cold.

Pretend to be happy.

Pretend to be happy.

Until I don't have to pretend anymore.

The Afterthought

You snap your fingers.

They come running.

You get what you want as soon as you ask.

If you needed me,

I was there.

I'm always there.

But, when are you there for me?

Your there when its convenient.

When you have to.

You help when you feel like it.

I feel like the afterthought.
And when I tell you the truth,
you victimize yourself.
You don't like to be wrong,
so you make me feel guilty.
Why is that?
Why don't you admit it?
I listen to you cry but I cry by myself.
I open my ears for you,
but you shut yours to me.
I can't talk to you,
so I talk to other people.
I'm scared of you.
I shouldn't be,
but you get so angry.
Why?
Why are you so angry?
Why do you make me feel small?
I cry by myself.
I don't let you in,
you didn't want to be apart before.

I hang out with them,

since you never wanted to hang out with

me.

You did your own thing.

You had tons of friends.

You had friends that didn't like me.

You talked about me behind my back

I knew it.

I'm not stupid and I'm not naive.

You treat me like a child.

You did you,

so I did me.

And I got use to that.

You justify why you do what you do.

Why I'm the afterthought.

Why you forget about me.

So now you're angry.

Your upset with the truth.

What now?

Guilt trip me.

Make this my fault.

Point out my flaws.

Not talk to me.

Ignore me for the billionth time.

I don't care.

I don't care anymore.

Until you prove me wrong.

Rage

Unpredictable, blinding, pain.

Emotions rising.

Bubbling over.

Intense feelings reign.

Repressed thoughts rise to the surface.

We say things we regret.

Overwhelmed and upset.

Pushed past the breaking point.

Rage divides us.

It takes away love,

Replacing it with hate.

A bitter taste.

Unnecessary waste.

It reveals your inner hurt.

The pain of your past.

Repressed emotions attached.

Feeding on Rage.

Perfection

Stand tall, don't slouch, smile, be cordial.

Don't let them see your flaws. Look the

part. Act like you know what you're doing.

Don't let them see you sweat. Don't cry.

Don't complain. Don't fail. They, can't see

you fail. They can't see the truth. Tell them

your fine. You're okay. You're doing great.

Lie. Tell them what they want to hear, keep

the other stuff to your self. Try to keep it

together. Play the part. Don't let them in.

Hide. Hide the insecurity. Hide the flaws.

Hide the struggle. Hide the fear. Keep it in a bottle. Stay in control. This is what they want. This is who they want to see. Give the people what they want. Perfection. No matter what. Cover your flaws. Dress up nice. Don't let them see the discomfort. Don't be weird. You have to keep it together, even when you want to cry. Stay calm, even when they offend you. Keep your mouth shut, even when you know their wrong. Cause you want them to like you. You want them to think your cool. You can handle it. Perfection.

Cracked

On the outside I am smiling, I am doing great. But the inside, is another story. There's a crack that I can't fix. It keeps leaking. My life has a crack in it that I don't know how to fix. I hide the crack with material things. Maybe new shoes will fix it. Or makeup, our an outfit. But that fades and reveals the crack again. The crack gets bigger every day. I find more creative ways to close the crack. I keep myself busy. I drink, I hang out, I work. But the crack won't heal. Its apart of me. I'm broken. I act like nothing is bothering me when everything is bothering me. I put on a brave face then go home and cry it away.

I'm scared, I'm only human. I overthink, I have bad dreams and bad thoughts. I crave attention, but I lack it. I want so much in life but lack the motivation. I want to be normal but my mind operates in the abnormal. I want to fast-forward and rewind all in the same time. Fix my past while fixing my future. I want success but it seems so difficult to obtain. I want to smile for real, all the time. Life has broken me. Now I have this huge crack. I fail, I make mistakes. I'm wrong. The crack tells the truth. The crack shows where I've been. Here I am now, cracked, but here.

Fear

Afraid of the dark, afraid the shadows, afraid of life. Too scared to live. Too scared to become my destiny. Holding back out of fear. Afraid of rejection, afraid of being different, afraid to stand out. Fear is at my throat. Fear has my mind. Living life in fear. Fear to be myself. I want to speak out. I want to be in the center. The life of the party. For once, I'd like to be the fun one. Have people genuinely want to be with me. But my fear. My fears control me, like a puppet. I cower to my room. I cry for the person I want to be. I yearn for the confidence I lack. I want to be bold. I want to be free of the fear. I want to live without set backs. I battle with my fear. Sometimes I win, sometimes I lose. If I have support with me, I find I can push back my fear.

Consumed

Sometimes we get so overwhelmed and wrapped up in our problems, that we forget everyone else. We forget to check in on friends and loved ones. We all have felt pain. We struggle with loss. We all worry. We have all cried tears of guilt regret and remorse. There is always someone out there with a bigger issue. Yet we single ourselves out like we are the only one in the world who has ever experienced heartache. We think we are the very first person to experience betrayal. We take it so heavy. We consume ourselves with our own problem to the point of mental breakdowns. We lose our minds over it. But everyone hurts. You're not alone in your journey. Get up, look around. The pity party stops here.

The Change

I am changing. I am shifting. Moving forward. Rising from the past. Shedding off the shame, the pain, the loss, the worry. I am becoming a new being. It has taken some time. I had to go through trials and test. I needed to work for it. I am still working. I am upgrading my lifestyle.

Tapping into my talents. I want to challenge myself. I need to embrace the new me. Like a rose blooming. Like a butterfly emerging from its cocoon. The time is important for me to flourish. My time is soon. My voice will break the walls I have been bound to. The words of these pages will speak to the souls who understand. I declare it. I am here. I am ready.

Triggered

There are certain words, and actions that can awake past trauma. Unintended. It's not your problem, it's mine. The mind has a way of remembering certain defense mechanisms that are not needed anymore.

They didn't mean to make me feel like this. They're not ignoring me. It's not like that anymore. I do not need to panic. But sometimes it feels like I'm back in the moment. I remember the rejection. I remember the pain. I remember it as if it's all over again. But it's not. Why am I so triggered by this. Why can't I let it go? I want to move on.

Chapter Three : Life

Out Of Hiding

In order to not be judged or called

out, I shed my identity and conformed. I

blended into the scenery. I did not want

confrontation. I did not wish to be called

out for simply being myself. So I hid myself

from the world. I took myself, my

thoughts, my opinions, my style, my voice,

from the world. I took it all away. I didn't

want the drama. I didn't want my

differences to clash. I didn't want to bother

anyone. I went away, mentally. I shut

down, logged out, and went into autopilot.

I didn't know how to handle my life. I

didn't know how to live, so I lived for

everyone else. Well, I guess it's time to

come out of hiding.

Little Girl

Just a little girl trying to figure out

life. Just trying to understand what's wrong

and what's right. Refusing to grow up too

fast. Holding on to the past. Scared to

move on. Fearful of the future. Just a little

girl trying to play it safe. Never starting

drama. Always avoiding trouble. A little girl

that lacked confidence. A little girl, afraid of

being wrong. So she stayed silent. She

conformed. She changed herself. Just to avoid rejection. She agreed to things She had no business fooling with. She was submissive. Poor scared little girl, escaping to her room, falling into her bed, and crying into her pillow. Energy drained. Confused in her identity. Nowhere to turn. All she had to cling to was her faith. Even that made her feel guilty. Just a little girl, looking for acceptance. Looking to feel appreciated. Sad little girl. She didn't love herself. She didn't like her shape. She didn't know what to do with her hair. And on top of that, she had acne. She didn't know her worth. She disrespected herself. She didn't want her life. She prayed to be taken away. Just a little girl. Trying to find

herself. Trying to find her voice.

Awkward

I don't know what to say. So I stay

silent. Scared to speak. Scared to be

wrong. Afraid that my voice may offend

you. I try to stay calm and quiet to

compensate for others. I don't know how to

be social. It's hard to fit in. Conversations

are awkward. If I can't relate, I don't say

anything. I nod and smile. Crowds make

me uncomfortable. I look down, avoid eye

contact, move quick, get in and get out. I

stay close to who I know. Stay to myself.

People don't understand it. They question

what they can't relate to. They assume my character because I don't talk a lot. I lack charisma so they ignore me. I am the outcast. I'm left alone. Me and my thoughts. Vulnerable. Open to be taken advantage of. I feel weak. Drawn to people who show me kindness. Never sure if they were using me or generally wanted to know me. I lost trust as I got older. I've been taken advantage of. I've put time and energy into relationships that failed. My walls stay up. Guarded. I stay quiet. Figuring out life on my own.

Introvert

"Why are you so quiet? Why don't you ever go out? You sit in the house all day. Why don't you talk? Your weird." Anti-social. I don't like confrontation. I have limits, social limits. An introvert prefers more alone time, not to say they are not social, they just need to recharge every now and then. I love my friends and my family. I love going out. I enjoy company. Just understand I need my space. Let me warm up first. Get to know me better. Don't assume my personality. I'm not stuck up, just shy. Just because I'm not talking doesn't mean I don't like you. I'm listening, I'm processing. I just don't know what to say yet. I may not be the conversation starter, but I can end it.

My Skin

Imagine this, you're a preteen black girl. You are trying to understand your body. You have yet to realize your true worth. You want to have smooth fair light skin. But there's something stopping you. Acne. You wash your face, smear on masks, creams, toners, but it doesn't quite work. So you manage. Some days are good, other days are nightmares. You look at the people around you. They all have smooth, clear skin. They barely break out. You wonder what they do to manage that.

You wonder what's wrong with you. You try to pop your bumps, but you end up with blemishes. Now you have acne and uneven skin. You feel ugly. You hate your skin. It makes you depressed, so you stop trying. Your skin gets worse. It's not going to change unless you stick to your routine. Suddenly, you get noticed. You realize, maybe your not that ugly. You're finally controlling your skin...for the most part. You start seeing a dermatologist. Your face starts to change little by little. Years go by and you realize your worth. You finally find people who have skin like you. You learn how to use makeup. You gain confidence. Now you look in the mirror and see your beauty, acne and all. You battle your

breakouts with grace. You appreciate your

brown skin. You embrace your blemishes.

This is me. This is my skin.

New School

Why don't they like me? What am I

doing wrong? Am I not pretty enough? I

don't talk enough. I'm not exciting. But If

they just let me in, I could show them. I'll

tell them about myself, no, no, I'd sound

stupid. What would I say? I have no idea

what to say. New place, new people, new

issues. I'm feeling overwhelmed. Now

they'll think I don't want to talk to them.

But I do. I just have no idea what they

want me to talk about. They don't ask me

questions like, what was your other school

like, or where are you from. They keep

asking me why don't I talk. Well, why don't

you start a conversation with me, and we'll

see what happens. If I have something to

say, I'll say it. I don't like it here. I don't

like uniforms. I don't like the feeling of

confinement. This is all new and weird. I'm

insecure. I feel pressured to be someone

that I am not. Just to fit in. Nobody wants

to talk to me. Is it me? Can't wait to get

out of here. Just have to endure it. At least

I can get some bible knowledge. English is

pretty good. And history is cool. But Math,

another story. I'll just keep my head down,

get my work done, so I can bust out of here. I met a few friends. I appreciate them for understanding me. A few nice teachers too. But I've got to get out of here. I don't quite like it here. It feels hypocritical. How can people go to a christian school and still be so cruel, stuck up and pretentious. Then the rumors that would spread. The craziest things done in the depths of this christian school. I want out. The count down till graduation begins.

Young "Love"

I learned about love through movies. I made unrealistic expectations. No one told me about red flags or warning signs. I wanted to have a movie love. I wanted it

so bad I blinded myself. I ignored the flags.

I thought that it would get better. I wanted

the dream. I wanted the fairy tale but I fell

into a nightmare. I felt betrayed after

feeling so sure. My actions and decisions

were all stupid. I should have known the

minute you opened your mouth. I saw it

happen in front of my eyes and I said

nothing. I let you get away with it. I stayed

quiet. My first mistake was waiting too long

to speak up. My second mistake was

allowing you to control me. When I finally

said my peace, it was too late. I wanted

out but you didn't understand. We were

beyond the limit, and I was afraid of you.

You couldn't let me go. Why couldn't you just let me go. Free me. Move on. Stop calling me. Stop threatening me. You cursed at me, called me names then turned right back around begging me to stay. This time you would not have your way. I told you I needed space, and you would not listen to me. You stalked me. Smiling at me like you never said you would kill yourself if I didn't take you back. You talked about suicide while I was dealing with the death of a family member. And you knew this, how selfish of you. You went and cried to others about me. How dare you. How dare you try to make yourself the victim. I'm the one who saw the real you. You lied to me and laughed in my face. You pressured me for things I was not ready for. You avoided my friends and family, and they saw what I tried to overlook. I gave you so much. I gave you so many chances. So many times I've tried to fix myself for you. You ignored my calls, my cries. You disrespected me. And when I finally found the strength to say no more, you became someone I never thought you could be. Sure we had fun times and you made me laugh, but it was not enough. I could not breathe. Your energy was too much for me. We were not meant to be. I'm sorry. It was a mistake that I needed to learn from. I hope you're better now. I hope you got the help you needed. I pray you find your path. Thank you. You taught me that if I don't speak up and say what's on my mind, I let people think they can get away with anything.

Loss

The pain experienced when losing a loved one is hard. It comes in unexpectedly. It feels like a hole has been punched into your chest. I have lost a lot of loved ones. At a time it seemed like every other year I was at a funeral. Back to back I faced loss. It seemed as though it was all happening during many crucial periods of my life such as, transitioning to a new school, puberty and senior year. Not only was I morning loss of loved ones, but I was also stressed, unsure of my path, and still trying to figure out my purpose. I experienced one of the hardest and most toxic break-ups during the loss of an uncle. The pain and trauma it gave me, I would not wish on anyone. We live our lives never wishing to hear of the loss of loved ones. We wish they could stay with us forever. We get so use to having them there that when its time for them to depart, it hurts to our core. All we have left are the memories, photographs, and the belongings. They are missed dearly. The amount of tears shed is uncontrollable and immeasurable. Their life is truly missed. Every now and then I hesitate when I attended funerals in support for my friends and family. I know what to expect. I feel their hurt, tears, and pain. I know what it's like to be in their place, so I empathize with what they are dealing with. My mind flashes back to the moments of hurt and loss I experienced, and I reflect on the pain. I know it hurt for me, so it's defiantly hurting for them too. Sometimes I don't want to go because I know that I will feel the pain again. Because I've been there so many times. Loss is hard. It hurts, but in time, you learn to fill the emptiness with love, memories, and appreciate the time you had with them. They may be gone, but their spirit still lives on.

Duffy

I always dreamed of having a pet. I would
beg and barging and plead my case as to
why I a needed and wanted one so badly.
I've had three pets so far. The first was a
black cockerspaniel named Pepper. He was
cute and fun to be with but he got
aggressive when it came to food. In the
end we had to give him up because of his
anger. After a couple of years, the second
pet that came into my life was a bunny
named snowball. She didn't last long. She
didn't sleep though the night, made a lot of
noise, pooped constantly, and ate my
favorite dolls face off. She was cute, but
she had red eyes that freaked me out at

times. We ended up having to send

Snowflake away. Finally after some years

past there was Duffy. He was named after

my granny's old dog. He was just a puppy

when I got him and I immediately fell in

love. I promised to myself that I would

always protect him and look after him. He

was full of love and energy. He was always

excited to see me walk through the door.

Always ready to play. And he never tried to

snap at me or bite me. He understood me

and tried his best to be a good boy.

Whenever I was sad, he would try to cheer

me up by licking my tears and whining at

me. He always knew when I needed a hug.

He was the best cuddle buddy. I had him

for eight years. When I found out he had kidney failure, I felt hopeless. Duffy was weak, he stopped eating, and he looked so miserable. I couldn't save him. I couldn't afford to save him. My heart was broken. There I was, in the veterinarian office, crying. Duffy was looking at me wondering what's happening to him. It was one of the hardest things I had to do. It was like losing my best friend. Who was going to be with me on my low days now? Who would keep me company? I was alone again. Having Duffy there helped fill the empty spots of my life. Now I just felt exposed. I was vulnerable again. Duffy had become my emotional support. He had become the

being I could rely on when no one would
listen. And now I had to force myself to
move on.

College

And now, I am finally able to find
myself. I'm finally able to be myself. I've
found people like me here. I've found the
outcast. They talk to me, they listen. They
welcome me. I can learn about what I love.
I can grow my craft to become
professional. It's hard, but I like it. I get
nervous but I'm okay. This is a good space.
I know who I am. I know what I want. I've
found out things about myself I never
knew. I'm growing through past hurt.

Moving though mistakes. Taking baby steps towards my goal. I finally feel like I belong. I can sit by myself without people questioning me. People sit with me. They like me. They see my talent. They can see me. They really see me. They understand. I feel accomplished. I get to spend my days in the theater. It's my playground. I love to be in it. I love being a part of it. I know the actors. They know me. I finally feel included. I finally feel needed. This is how I want to feel for the rest of my life. I want these moments to never leave. College showed me what it takes. It helped me come out of my shell. I've surprised myself. I'm proud of myself.

Fibroids

I woke up one day and noticed a
mass in my abdomen. It was hard. It was
weird. When I went to the bathroom, I
thought it was gone. It was small and
almost undetectable. I went on with life
thinking maybe its just my bladder. A year
went by and it was bigger. I was fat. I
looked like I was pregnant. It was still hard
and I became nervous. My face would
break out terribly. My periods were so
heavy, I needed to use four overnight pads
for one day. Each one heaver than the
next. What was going on in my body? I
worried, and feared the for the worse. I
was scared of what the doctor would tell

me. I finally set my appointment almost

mid-year. It was time to get the truth.

Possible fibroid. I had to get an ultra-sound

to be sure. I had multiple doctor

appointments and a new gynecologist. It

was so weird getting an ultra-sound. It was

like I was having a baby. But I was not.

Interior: cold, dim lit room with huge

machine. It was scary but the nurse was

nice. But it was very quiet. By my next

appointment it was confirmed. Fibroids the

size of a grapefruit. It was hereditary. My

mom had a hysterectomy because of it.

Was this my fate? My fear grew. "Lord, I

want to have kids." I prayed. I was

reassured that my fibroids grew on the

outside, and they would simply go in and cut them off. No hysterectomy, relief for now. My gynecologist, the one who would remove the fibroids explained her process to me but warned of a possible ovary removal. The fear was back as I waited anxiously for the surgery date. I was getting the fibroids removed, but what if they take more? I would have to recover for six weeks. Sitting, not working. How are my bills going to get paid? Worrying. What's going to happen? The day had finally come and I cried, prayed, cried, and prayed some more. My friends and family prayed, and now the day had come. I fell asleep comfortable but woke up in pain.

What had they done? The world was fuzzy and I was in pain. Where am I? The nurses talked about me and to me but I couldn't understand what they were saying. Then there was the dizzy trip to my room, bumping into walls. I know I looked mad. But I was in pain. I'm sorry I looked so irritated, but it hurt. The pain starts to fade with the help of morphine, scary. I felt so drugged but I could still understand my moms voice. "They only removed the fibroids, everything is still in tact!" I was so relieved I wanted to cry. It's finally over. I get to keep my dream. I later realized, they had put me on the floor with all the new mothers. Most of these women had

given birth to babies, and me, I had
fibroids. I survived, and now it was time to
recover.

In That Moment

In that moment, I felt helpless. In
that moment, I felt alone. In that moment
I felt invisible. Heartache. Hopeless. Unsure
how to grasp my feelings. Overwhelmed
with emotion. Unsure if I was overreacting
or if the thoughts can be validated. In that
moment the tears would not stop, my
thoughts were racing, and my mind
became a prison. In that moment, I had to
fight for my sanity back. I got lost in the
moment. I struggle with these moments.

They haunt me. I'm never sure what will

trigger the moment. I must find control.

When the moment comes, I must

overcome it. I want to be stronger than it. I

want to know what to do in the moment. In

that moment I will survive it. In that

moment I will find myself.

Thoughts of Suicide

What would they say? What would

they do? If I followed through and I gave

into my thoughts. What would happen? If I

decided to give in and I let my thoughts

control me. Where would that take me?

What could have become of me? There are

moments in my life where it has felt as

though I have hit rock bottom. I have been

so low. I wonder how many people have

felt this feeling. It feels like a nightmare.

It's a nightmare that you want to wake up

from, but you are already awake. So how

do you escape? How do you escape the

mental haunting? What do I need to do to

get this out of my head? I'm suffering in

my silence. I am screaming in my head. A

desperate cry for help, only I won't admit it

to you. I am ashamed. I shouldn't be like

this. So do I cut my life short to get it over

with? Should I down some pills to

overdose? I couldn't go through with it. I'm

too much of a wuss. So now I'm upset with

myself because I don't want to be here, but

I'm too scared to take my own life. What do you do? Who do you talk to? I guess I'll talk to you. I've been hiding a lot of things from people. I've put on a mask and costume. I have fooled them into thinking I'm normal. But, I am not. Something is not right. I have experienced slight trauma in my past. My mind makes me want to feel sad. I don't want to move. I cry. I hurt inside. I am reminded of all my mistakes. I fear. I feel unaccomplished. I feel plain. I feel like a mistake. I go through life as a ghost. No one acknowledges me, or cares to ask or even listen. I'm just going along for the ride. Drifting from sanity. Sinking into despair. But do you even care? Is this depression? Am I okay? Does any one else feel like this. Hello??? Am I alone? Can anyone relate? Can someone just understand? Sometimes I feel so sad. Is this what mental illness is?

The Man After Gods Own Heart

When you grow up in a christian household, you are bound to learn about every story in the bible. Two of my favorite people were Joseph and David. David was fascinating to me because no matter what he did, God still loved him. David praised God through the good and the bad. In the bible, the book of psalms has letters from David. He described his joy, his pain, his fear, and his pride. He gave praise where it was due and his passion was so intense. If David can live through what he did, surely I can get through as well. I want to have this much passion in my writing. I want to be after Gods heart, like David. David was a blessed and anointed man. He taught me how to express my feelings and handle what I'm going through. It takes great faith. I need great faith to take me to the next level.

P.U.S.H.

Somewhere along the line, I guess I forgot to keep pushing. I decided I was not worth it. I stopped my push. Pray until something happens. I let other people push for me. I got lazy. I lost hope. I got impatient. I tried to do my own thing. I forgot the important part of P.U.S.H. That's the U. Pray *Until* something happens. Never stop praying. I should never stop. I need to pray until the miracle happens. Pray until the heavens come down. Pray until your blessings come. And when that happens, keep praying. I just have to keep pushing. You just have to keep pushing. Even when it seems hopeless, push. When it looks bad, push. When you're in trouble, push. When it feels like your in a "now what" stage, push. Pray until something happens.

The Virus that Shook the World

Its 2019, December 31. Our hearts are hopeful, our dreams are big. Young and hungry. Making plans for the future. We were all excited and planning big. Then January came, we thought we had time. We saw it happening, but we didn't know what to expect. We were trying to thrive. February brought the first known signs. We could see what it was doing and no one knew how to stop it. By March, panic had set in. The world was suffering from a virus called COVID-19. A virus that was stealing the breath of its victims. A virus that spread so fast, there was no time to grieve, no time to heal, no time to realize whether you had it or not. No vaccine in sight. You would either survive or you don't. Just like that, plans where cancelled. We were quarantined. No one could visit, no one could leave. We were separated from family and friends. Our goals were set back. Our hopes were crushed. The world stopped. All we could wonder was if this was the end. Sickness and death passed through each state, each country, each continent. It became inescapable. For four months, we stayed still. We prayed, and waited. It's June, but we are still in a pandemic. People are slowly trying to adapt. We wear mask and sanitize every three minutes. We get tested and check our temperatures daily. We are trying to stay positive in the new normal. We are extra precautious when we go out. We keep our distance. Working from home is the new normal. Homeschool is the new normal. Lysol is now a rare commodity. We are surviving. Every month brings new adjustments. Malls don't stay open too long now. Restaurants rely on takeout orders. Small businesses are struggling to stay alive. The economy is trying not to fall. Through all the madness, we overcome. Through all of the chaos this virus brought, we still overcome. We are already building ourselves up. When it's all over, we will thrive again.

2020

This is for the nurse who can't find
the will to pick herself up from the floor
after seeing so much hurt, pain, struggle
and death. This is for the husband who has
to find the will to live after losing his best
friend. This is for the one who feels
detached and separated from their loved
ones. I pray life and hope for you. This is
for the fearful, the stressed, the confused,
the lonely. I speak life, comfort and love to
you. This is for the sick, the weary, and the
ones standing close to the edge. Don't give
up the fight. We are strong. I pray you
have hope in a bright future ahead. I pray
we remember all the good memories to

help us rest our heads. I pray we humble ourselves and look to God for help. When it seems like a never ending sad story, I want us to change our mindset. Find joy in the little things. As we battle against keeping our sanity, I pray that we win. I hope we learn life lessons. I hope we accept ourselves for who we are. I pray we find love in ourselves. In this time of chaos, I pray for your peace to be found, your faith renewed, and for miracles to take place.

Emotional

I just wanted a hug every now and then. I needed that kind of love. I needed assurance. I needed to be held. Sometimes

I can't help but cry, but growing up, I was told to be stronger. I was told I shouldn't cry over everything. My tears even made some angry and frustrated with me. They thought I could cry on command. They thought I was too much. I was a crybaby. My emotions were misunderstood. I had to hide my tears to make people feel comfortable. I hid my tears to show I wasn't weak. I kept it all back. Unable to feel, unable to express. Unsure of how to emote. I could not be vulnerable with anyone. I dare not let someone see me shed a tear. I controlled it so well that I rarely shed a tear in public. It became embarrassing to me. After all of those years of bottled up emotion, it started to become harder to keep a straight face. I started to experience emotional breakdowns over minor inconveniences. I could not understand what was going on with me. I would cry uncontrollably. As much as I tried to stop it, it continued to overwhelm me. I became undone. I became an emotional wreck. I could never escape the fact that I am an emotional being. Crying is my release. I never forced myself to cry. My feelings are real. Being told to "suck it up", "stop", "fix your face", and "get yourself together" left mental scars on me. Hiding my emotions has turned into an abuse on myself by not letting me feel what I'm going through. I have to cry in private so I don't cause someone to feel uncomfortable. Crying in private, wishing to be held, for encouragement, a positive gesture. I just really needed a hug. Thats all.

Chapter Four: Love Letters

I John 4:16,21

"And we have known and believed
the love that God hath to us. God is love;
and he that dwelleth in love dwelleth in
God, and God in him. And this
commandment have we from him, That he
who loveth God love his brother also."

Dear Younger Me

Dear younger me,

If I ever had the opportunity to meet
you, I would hug you so tight. Because, I
know you need it. Every day, you needed
it. You are a strong black woman who

needs validation from no one. Remember who you are. You are not a screw-up, or a disappointment. You are loved. You don't have to change to be loved. Your flaws are beautiful, no matter what they say. Please be careful what you pray for. Because you have to be ready for it. You really have to focus. But don't let go of that beautiful imagination. Write that kids book. Finish those plays. And try not to procrastinate too much. They need to be seen and read. You will be heard. Stand up for yourself. You have so much confidence in you. Younger me, you matter, and you're going to make it. Keep on marching to your beat. You will find people who accept you no matter what. If you're hurting, tell them.

Speak up. It's going to be okay. Never lose

sight of your dream. Continue to pray, and

seek the Lord daily. It gets better. No

matter what, stay patient and keep

pressing forward. You are not alone. Don't

doubt yourself and don't doubt God. His

presence is always near. I love you, and I

always will, no matter what mistakes were

made.

Thankful

I will still be thankful. I will praise God

through my good and my bad. Because He

has something beautiful in store for me and

I can't wait to get there. I will be thankful

through my struggle, through, the
heartache, and though the loneliness. I will
stay faithful even when it feels like God's
not there. I will be patient and wait for my
harvest. I will sow these seeds in faith
knowing that a great harvest is coming. No
matter what, I will keep my faith.

Way Maker

I can't escape Your miracles. God,
you are amazing. You hear my needs and
answer prayers. Even when I whine, You
hear me. Through my highs and lows.
Through loss and pain, You have always
been there. You are a way maker. You can
do anything. I've witnessed Your works.

You can do the impossible. That is why I believe. I have faith. Through every trial, I have survived because of you. I've had dark times. I've had moments where I have felt unwanted and unnecessary. But You make me important. You gave me purpose. God, You are everything. Nothing is impossible for You. Thank You for Your mercy and grace. Because of You, I can write this book, and I will finish strong.

Psalm 8:3-5 (King James Version)
"When I consider thy heavens, the work of thy fingers, the moon and the stars, which thou has ordained; What is man, that thou art mindful of him? And the son of man,

that thou visitest him? For thou has made him a little lower than the angels, and hast crowned him with glory and honour."

Self Love

I am on a journey. I'm figuring myself out. I never really knew, how to love myself. I abused myself. I filled my head with negative thoughts. I hated myself. I hated how I looked. I couldn't see. I was blinded by all the flaws. Acne, scars, uneven skin-tone, frizzy hair and crooked teeth. I did not know how to embrace my flaws. I tolerated myself. If you told me I was pretty, I would think you were just trying to be nice. I did not understand my beauty.

Ten years later, I think I understand. I look in the mirror and see the black queen I was meant to be.

II Corinthians 1:3,4

"Blessed be God, even the Father of our Lord Jesus Christ, the Father of mercies, and the God of all comfort. Who comforteth us in all our tribulation, that we may be able to comfort them which are in any trouble, by the comfort wherewith we ourselves are comforted of God."

Mother

She is strong. She carries the weight of the world. She gives birth and nurtures.

She works hard and strives for the best for her children. She wakes up before the sun and doesn't sleep until her work is done. She is a mother, a teacher, a stylist, chief, an accountant, a therapist, a friend, a survivor, a mother. She is confident, loving, kind, caring, generous, faithful. She is a woman. She deserves the world.

The Open Door

I can see it now.

I can see the open door.

I see the endless possibilities.

All I have to do is claim it and believe.

It was open the whole time.

I blinded myself.

I kept my own self from the truth.

I doubted it.

It was only something I could imagine.

But now reality is setting in.

It is possible to achieve my goals.

I understand myself better now.

Everything I go through is only

preparation.

I want to go through the open door.

I want to see the other side.

I want to see what is in store for me.

I can do it.

As I approach this door, I still fear.

But I will embrace my destiny.

I choose to put myself out there.

I choose to be vulnerable.

The door is open.

A Vow

You brought my imagination back. I feel free when I am with you. There are no limits when we are together. My spirits are lifted, my hope is restored. I finally found true happiness, and I found it in you. You know how to talk to me. Although you give me my space, I still want you to occupy it. I need to touch your face, and hold you to make sure your real. I need to make sure your not just imagination. When I need you, you are there. You are the calm in my storm. You come in and give me peace. You inspire my dreams. Wherever you are, that's where I want to be. I love you. My

heart is on my sleeve. My feelings are here,

served to you on a silver platter. You have

me in your hands. My heart flutters when I

see you. I can't help but smile every time,

even when I want to be upset. You make

me smile. I look goofy in love. Dare I look

into those eyes, I may be lost forever. Your

kindness is overwhelming. You care about

me more than yourself. I want you to have

everything you've dreamed of having. I

want to give you so much. I prayed for you

to come, and you were here all along. I

pray we grow stronger and achieve our

goals. I want to be by your side through it

all.

Blessed

I've been blessed with a big family. A comfortable house. Healthy lifestyle. Why should I feel depressed? I have friends, talents, a good education, and the ability to learn more. Why should I be discouraged? I am loved. People look out for me. My family cares about my decisions. Why should I feel alone? I have had high moments and I have had low moments. But the highs have far outweighed the bad. I have had setbacks, but I have also had comebacks. I struggle, but I succeed in the end. I am still here. I am truly blessed to still be here. I have been able to help people. I have been a blessing to many.

Whenever I am needed, I try my best. I am needed. I have importance. Why stay in dark places when there is so much beauty to be created and found in the light? Step out of the dark hole of drama and despair. Remember your blessings. Remember Who created you.

Let Go

It's time to shed myself of these thoughts and emotions. It's time to breathe in and breathe out then move on. No more pity party. No more sadness. Time to stand up and let it go. I said what I said. I spoke my peace. And now you know. The old me would want you to stay sorry for me. But I am over it now. It's in the past. Depression

will no longer hold me. Fear will not be my

enemy. Guilt can not control me anymore.

This is the season of never looking back.

This is the season of moving forward.

Stepping into the unknown. Breathing easy.

Smiling genuinely. Laughing for real. I will

own my confidence. I will not be stopped. I

wrote it down. I read it to myself. And now,

I will let it go. Goodbye little girl. I can not

hold on to you anymore. I am releasing my

past to gain my future. I have to find my

way. I need to keep my faith. As long as

God is still a promise keeper, I have

nothing to worry about.

I Love Me

I Love me because God created me special.

I am a unique brand, a very rare find.

I love the way I smile.

It's so big that it reaches my eyes, making

them smile.

I love my hair.

Its soft yet wild, flexible yet untamable. It

challenges me and give me a good arm

workout.

I love my eyes.

They let me see the beauty, nature and

people.

I love my body.

Its strong enough to handle my reckless

moments, it curves naturally, and it allows

me to move daily.

I love my mind.

It contains all kinds of knowledge, helps

me make decisions, and lets me control my

destiny.

I love myself.

I choose to put me first. I love the flaws

that help me learn and grow. I love the

imperfections that humble me. I love the

emotions that help me understand and

connect with others. I love the God that

made me for purpose. I love that I can

express these feelings knowing that

someone out there who reads this can

smile and relate.

Love yourself, be yourself, embrace it and

never turn back.

Affirmations

Today, I will be strong.

I can do this.

I have been blessed with another day.

I am loved.

I am forgiven.

I do not need to worry about the past.

My future is very bright.

I am in Gods hands.

The Lord watches the sparrow, so I know

He watches me.

I will have peace.

I declare victory in the name of Jesus.

God keeps all his promises.

I am not alone.

I am fearfully and wonderfully made.

Now It's Your Turn

Pull out your pen. Turn on your laptop.
Sharpen your pencils. Find a good
notebook. Write it down. Whatever it is on
the inside that's pulling on you. Write it
out. Draw it out. Speak it. Let it be known
in the atmosphere. Get it off your chest.
Then, let it go. Give yourself a daily
affirmation or a daily devotion to get you
through. Pray until something happens.